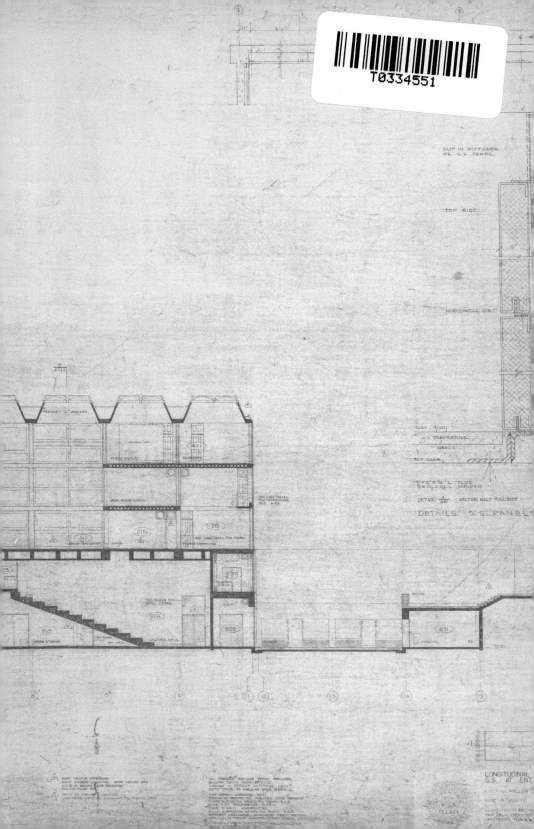

The series *On Center* explores the collections, history, and professional activities of the Yale Center for British Art, the largest collection of British art outside the United Kingdom.

Library of Congress Cataloging-in-Publication Data

Names: Prown, Jules David, author. | Kahn, Louis I., 1901–1974.
Title: The late architectural philosophy of Louis I. Kahn as expressed in
  the Yale Center for British Art / Jules David Prown.
Description: New Haven : Yale Center for British Art, [2020] Series:
  On center ; v. 1 | Summary: "The fundamentals of Kahn's architectural
  philosophy begin with his personal history: his inherent talent; his
  family background and childhood experiences; his education, from
  elementary school through architectural school; the influences of Paul
  Philippe Cret and Beaux Arts architecture; and his travels, especially
  those to study the antique monuments of Egypt, Greece, and Rome.
  Because the causal aspects of these experiences were absorbed by him,
  rather than being the products of Kahn's own thinking, he rarely acknowledged them. His conclusions led to a philosophy that echoed some of the
  thoughts of earlier philosophers, like Spinoza and Heidegger, but were
  arrived at independently.1 Kahn expressed his philosophy in lectures,
  seminars, writings, interviews, conversation, and often through
  sketches. However, he habitually expressed himself elliptically—his
  phrasing poetic, his metaphors original and apt. Therefore, his meaning
  was often felt rather than understood. Extensive studies of Louis Kahn's
  architecture exist, but few focus on his fully developed architectural
  philosophy.2 This text addresses that subject, incorporating his own
  words (in italics) and relating them where relevant to his final work,
  the Yale Center of British Art (hereafter, "the Center"). Kahn died
  during the construction of the building, the last material expression of
  his architectural philosophy. I was the first director of the Center, a
  participant in the selection of the architect and throughout the
  building's planning and creation. Coincidental with the early years of
  Kahn's planning for the Center, two young architectural historians—
  John Cook and Heinrich Klotz—interviewed several leading architects,
  including Kahn. Working with a verbatim transcript of the Kahn
  interviews, made by Karen Denavit, I produced an edited version of the
  interviews in book format. Louis I. Kahn in Conversation: Interviews
  with John W. Cook and Heinrich Klotz (hereafter, "Kahn in Conversation")
  is the source for many of the Kahn quotations included here. A
  researcher can consult the full, verbatim transcript of the interviews
  in the Center's Institutional Archives, in the Manuscripts and Archives
  collections in Sterling Memorial Library at Yale University, and in the
  Architectural Archives of the University of Pennsylvania"—Provided
  by publisher.
Identifiers: LCCN 2020037065 | ISBN 9780300255287 (cloth)
Subjects: LCSH: Kahn, Louis I., 1901–1974—Aesthetics. | Architecture,
  Modern—20th century—Philosophy. | Yale Center for British Art.
Classification: LCC NA737.K32 P76 2020 | DDC 720.92—dc23
LC record available at https://lccn.loc.gov/2020037065

Designed by Lyn Bell Rose
Printed in Germany

Inside cover: Second project (detail), longitudinal section drawing,
April 3, 1974, Entrance Court and Library Court. Louis I. Kahn Collection,
The University of Pennsylvania and the Pennsylvania Historical
and Museum Commission

On Center
The Late Architectural Philosophy of Louis I. Kahn as Expressed in the Yale Center for British Art

Jules David Prown

YALE CENTER FOR BRITISH ART, NEW HAVEN
YALE UNIVERSITY PRESS, NEW HAVEN AND LONDON

Introduction

The fundamentals of Kahn's architectural philosophy necessarily begin with his personal history: his inherent talent, his family background and childhood experiences, his education from elementary school through architectural school, the influences of Paul Philippe Cret and Beaux Arts architecture, and his travels, especially those to study the antique monuments of Egypt, Greece, and Rome. Because the causal aspects of these experiences were absorbed rather than products of his own thinking, Kahn rarely acknowledged them. His conclusions led to a philosophy that echoed some of the thoughts of earlier philosophers like Spinoza and Heidegger but was arrived at independently.[1] Kahn expressed his philosophy in lectures, seminars, writings, interviews, conversation, and often through sketches. However, he habitually expressed himself elliptically—his phrasing poetic, his metaphors original and apt. Therefore, his meaning was often felt rather than understood.

Extensive studies of Louis Kahn's architecture exist, but few focus on his fully developed architectural philosophy (see page 42). This text addresses that subject, incorporating his own words (which appear in italics) and relating them where relevant to his final work: the Yale Center of British Art (hereafter, "the Center"). Kahn died during the construction of the building, the last material expression of his architectural philosophy. I was the first director of the Center and a participant both in the selection of the architect and throughout the building's planning and creation.

Coincidental with the early years of Kahn's planning for the Center, two young architectural historians—John Cook and Heinrich Klotz— interviewed several leading architects, including Kahn. Working with a verbatim transcript of the Kahn interviews made by Karen Denavit, I produced an edited version in book format, *Louis I. Kahn in*

Left to right: Jules Prown, Paul Mellon, and Kenneth Froeberg, April 11, 1974. Louis I. Kahn Collection, Manuscripts and Archives, Yale University Library

Conversation: Interviews with John W. Cook and Heinrich Klotz, which is the source for all of the Kahn quotations included here.

The source page numbers are cited sequentially on page 41. A researcher can consult the full verbatim transcript of the interviews in the Center's Institutional Archives, in the Manuscripts and Archives collections in Sterling Memorial Library at Yale University, and in the Architectural Archives of the University of Pennsylvania.

For Louis Kahn, creating architecture was more than simply designing a building to satisfy requirements specified by a client. He approached each commission from a broader perspective, based on his thoughts about the nature of the universe. An investigation into Kahn's original philosophy necessarily begins with his concept of eternity, embracing both physical manifestations and whatever may exist beyond our sensory capacities.

Louis Kahn during the construction of the Yale Center for British Art in February 1973.
Institutional Archives, Yale Center for British Art

View of the fourth-floor galleries

PRESENCE | SILENCE

What is has always been, yet has to await its realizations to give it presence.... Suppose it's for tomorrow instead of today. 'What is has always been.'... and so yesterday is also in today.

FIG 1: Louis I. Kahn, *Silence and Light*, original sketchbook drawing, ca. 1969. Louis I. Kahn Collection, The University of Pennsylvania and the Pennsylvania Historical and Museum Commission

For Kahn, the phrase "what is has always been" refers to an abstract realm, accessible to the human mind, where all possibilities exist— a concept akin to Plato's *Realm of Ideas*.

Kahn sometimes referred to that place as "Silence," sometimes as the "Inspirations," the "Sanctuary of Art," or the "Treasury of the Shadows."

He believed that the fundamental task of the architect should be to enter that realm, find an optimum solution to the problem posed by the program, and carry it across a threshold into Light, the "giver of all presences," to bring it into existence.[2]

> *Presence against existence. Somebody has to [realize it]. . . . Nothing can really be given presence unless it already is potentially possible to make it present.*

FACT AND TRUTH

> *Truth is different from fact. Nature's laws are based on fact. . . . Truth is psychological fact. . . . Truth has to do with desire.*

Kahn considered each thing or condition present in the physical universe—a brick, gravity, sunlight—as a fact. Truth, however, is reached through human imagination and transcends the facts of the natural world.

> *Everything I make must obey the laws of nature. But everything I will . . . is something that nature cannot do. Nature cannot make a house.*

The architect in practice should first search for and take advantage of facts related to his project, consider what is available in the natural world that can be used, and then go beyond the facts to find truth.

*Then you say, 'How do I put it into being?' You must . . .
immediately turn to nature . . . and say, 'I want to make this
thing, like you made me.'*

*Nature says, 'Okay now, you put this together, together,
together, you'll make it.' Nature will tell you. If you want
something that nature can't make, it'll tell you also. 'Can't
make it.' But then, make it. Man then . . . through his sense of
order. . . . makes through his own predilections, something.*

Kahn believed that the potential of a program often goes beyond the
client's perceived needs but can be envisioned and realized by the
architect, with or without the client's knowledge or understanding.
The architect can proceed to a place to which nature does not itself
provide the way.

*The program that comes to you . . . becomes transformed
because you see the needs in it, and you see that which has
not been at all expressed.*

*You just don't take it from the person, but you take it from
the way of life. . . . the way of life which commissions you.
. . . You are designing it for the person, but you are
designing it also for the person who will take it after this
person. . . . There only can be the expression of an era.*

DESIRE

We don't know all the laws in the universe except through desires. Through desires we know the needs. The needs are that which somehow has its ultimate goal in discovering the nature of desires. It is what man really seeks.

Kahn attached great importance to what he called desire, wish, or fairy tale.

The wish in the fairy tale is our inheritance of the first desires.

'Wish' grew out of the fact that there was no technology, and also no apparent experience from which a material expected to be found.... The fact that a man can wish is just so incredible. He knows very well that he's not going to fly just by saying so, but still he must satisfy that appetite.

When you're designing ... you make rules about the use of nature, which is law.... inspiring design to shape presence. The merging of desire and rule.

Kahn believed that desire has been fundamental to human achievement ever since our primordial ancestors. He believed that the desire to see led to the development of eyes.

If somebody told me that you see objects because light makes objects visible, and if you were to tell me also that the eyes were made because you have such a great desire to see what you feel, now I think it's what happened.... From the mere wanting to feel what you felt once that was particular, and want to feel it again ... sets up a kind of thing which gives you eyesight.

The day and the night, maybe, and the anticipation of the light which may have been giving you warmth ... sets up in nature that which gave living things eyesight."

HONESTY

*If men were shorter, if we were small as a bee,
I could make it much less.*

A fundamental aspect of Kahn's architectural philosophy was a commitment to honesty, truth. In his view, the way in which a building was constructed should be visible or deducible, both inside and out.

The columns on the exterior of the Yale Center for British Art express how the building was made, how it is held up. The outside walls present a sequence of 20-foot bays—ten on the front and back, six on the sides—marked by columns at 10-foot intervals. As they rise and carry less weight, the columns, as honest expressions of those facts, become narrower and recede from the beams. Similarly, the beams are much thicker where they span two columns and bear more weight.

Rather than reflecting an abstraction like symmetry, the exterior of the building truthfully expresses interior function. Glass windows allow daylight for offices and reading rooms; steel panels (which Kahn sometimes referred to as "opaque windows") imply solid interior gallery walls, staircases, library shelving, etc. At one point on the Center's facade, right of center, the beam supporting the third floor disappears for three bays, indicating that something different is happening inside: a two-story library reading room with study carrels at windows. Similarly, interior columns and the metal mechanical shafts in the middle of the building, which carry water, conditioned air, and electricity, become smaller as they rise and do less work.

The Library Court on the second floor is dominated by a cylindrical staircase that rises almost to but does not engage the V-Beams that support the roof. If it did, it would misleadingly appear to be a column supporting the roof rather than what it is, a freestanding staircase, a place of circulation and entrance.

FIG 2: Chapel Street facade

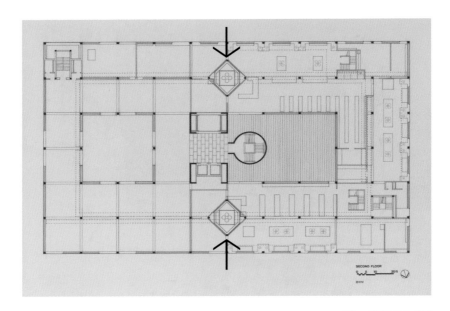

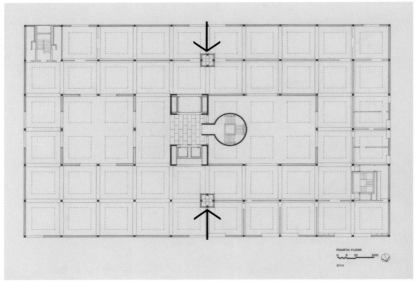

FIG 3: Second- and fourth-floor plans showing diamond and square mechanical-shaft shapes (in the center). Louis I. Kahn Collection, The University of Pennsylvania and the Pennsylvania Historical and Museum Commission

In adherence to Kahn's principle of honesty, defects that occurred in the process of construction or subsequently—stains in the concrete and breaks in the beads where forms met during the pour—are retained as testimony to the history of the building.

Kahn felt that a room was the most important of all architectural spaces.[3] The first plans for the Center had a space in the northwest corner of the building identified only as "The Room," a principle place for conversation and the exchange of ideas—in this case, eventually

FIG 4: Second floor, Library Court staircase cylinder and V-Beams

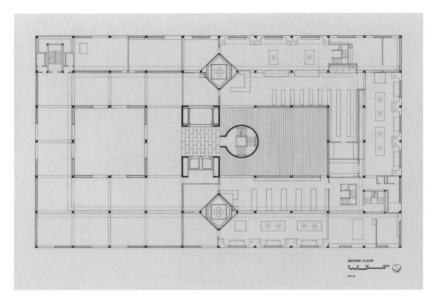

FIG 5: Fourth-floor plan. Louis I. Kahn Collection, The University of Pennsylvania and the Pennsylvania Historical and Museum Commission

serving as a conference room adjacent to the director's office. He felt that to qualify as a room, a place must have daylight in addition to enclosure; otherwise it was just a space or an area. Columns throughout express the 20-foot square-bay system, providing the opportunity to create single-bay rooms that Kahn considered to be a size that humans find comfortable. Removable partitions ("pogo panels") set on strips of travertine, running column to column, can define single-bay rooms or be spaced at will to create larger rooms.

All the materials in the Center are natural: travertine, steel, concrete, oak, wool carpeting, linen wall covering, etc. Nothing is painted, dyed, stained, or cosmeticized in any way. Kahn did not rank materials in a hierarchy of value. His concern was that a material be used honestly, in accordance with its nature. Under these terms, he accepted combinations of materials, like plywood with cinderblock. He loved brick for its ability to support and create walls, arches, etc., but it could not by itself make a lintel. Iron and steel could, however, and he honored that characteristic; he particularly liked to combine these materials in reinforced concrete because of what the combination could do.

SPENT LIGHT

Mountains, spent light. . . . streams, spent light. . . . all living things . . . microbes, leaves, trees, men. . . . came from what you might call eternity.

Fundamental to an understanding of Kahn's mature architectural philosophy is his conclusion that material is spent light. He knew that this idea was scientifically unacceptable—this was not a scientific truth but a poetic truth— and so cautioned his audience not to listen to scientists.

It seems as though you can be attacked by scientists more violently, but it's just the fairy tale. It is the power of the wish. . . . A wish is a terrific thing because a wish somehow precedes the means. . . . Therefore it's free really to move with one step from here to China. And no other way.

It could even be that you would never have to put a roof on a building. . . . Right now there is no evidence of that. . . . But, I don't like to say that it cannot be done . . . because its nature being nonconscious, it can really happen, but there you will give yourself to the universe when you are in the realm of the making of the material. . . . It's one of the manifestations of eternity.

LIGHT

Structure is the giver of the light. The structure gives light because it's where the structure is and the light is not.

Daylight pervades the Center. Light pours into the Entrance Court through clear skylights. In areas of the building where vulnerable works of art are shown, it enters through lighting that incorporates ultraviolet filtering.

All of the artificial lighting in the building was originally incandescent, which most closely approximated the color of daylight. Kahn worked on the Center in partnership with his lighting consultant, Richard Kelly, with whom he had recently collaborated at the Kimbell Art Museum, where daylight was also a top priority. Kelly had a theory, not universally accepted, that the daylight most damaging to works of art, because of ultraviolet radiation, came from the sun in the south and was deflected by the earth's atmosphere into the north sky, which was therefore bluer. Consequently, he designed a skylight system that blocked light coming from the north.[4]

The light that passes through those skylights is slightly more golden or yellow in hue than pure daylight because the blue ultraviolet is largely filtered out. The appearance of art and people illuminated by that light is, if anything, enhanced.[5]

FIG 6: Fourth floor, diffuser cassettes

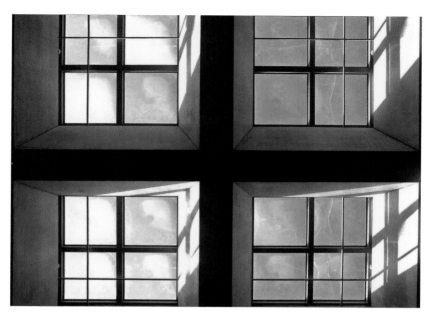

FIG 7: First floor, clear skylights in Entrance Court

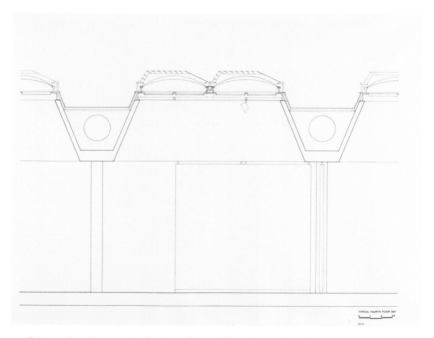

FIG 8: Second project, section drawing of fourth-floor bay, roof, and skylights.
Louis I. Kahn Collection, The University of Pennsylvania and the Pennsylvania Historical
and Museum Commission

FIG 9: View from Entrance Court to skylights, showing interior walls of second, third, and fourth floors. The third floor is light locked.

ORNAMENT

It was ornament, but not decoration. . . . It was an ornamentation of the joint, of the event.

Kahn disliked the word "decoration," perhaps because of its proximity to the concept of cosmeticizing or disguising. He believed that the decoration of a building, which he preferred to call "ornament," should not be applied but instead should be expressed by the structure. He felt that every architectural entity—columns, beams, walls, floor, ceiling, panels, bays, shafts, ducts, light tracks— should have their own identities, separate from anything else. To accomplish this would, of course, be structurally impossible. The building would not stand if its elements were not connected, but, with subtle recessions and protrusions, the independence of each unit in the Center is made manifest. Columns are separated from beams with a slight recess, often creating a darker area that works as a subtle capital. Similarly, columns visually stand apart from adjoining walls and from the floor. Incisions separate the wooden panels in the walls from their stiles and rails, echoing the vertical lines on the facade that define the edges of the adjacent panels of glass windows and steel.

Encircling lines on the staircase cylinder in the Library Court—deeper and broader than the lines demarcating the wooden forms used in construction—indicate each floor level. Protruding beads (including breaks) where the forms did not completely meet as the concrete was poured remain as ornament, as do the holes that were left when the tie-rods holding the forms were removed.

FIG 10: Second floor, Library Court details showing breaks and lines

ORDER

Order is the way of nature in the making of all things. In other words, order itself is the embodiment of all laws. And laws are different from rules. Man makes rules, nature is governed by laws. Laws are unchangeable. Rules are changing . . .

Psychological order is based on rules. Physical order is based on the nature of nature. In physical order, every grain of sand is the right size, the right color, the right place. The right weight. . . . There's no such thing as chaos in physical order. . . . Even an explosion is a manifestation of order.

A man. . . . thinks in terms of chaos. But that's not chaos. It's man not understanding, not comprehending.

Thus far, we have considered Kahn's personal philosophy without reference to the unspoken influence of what he learned in school, from his travels, from other architects, and from his reading. He left a visual trail of these influences in drawings, watercolors, pastels, and paintings while recording what caught his eye and mind and imagination, especially during his travels in the Near East and Europe.

Kahn did credit certain specific influences. The work of the architect Le Corbusier, whom Kahn admired, embodied much of what Kahn had learned in his travels about the basic forms that gave classical architecture its universal appeal for people throughout the ages.

Every man has . . . a figure in his work who he feels answerable to. I often say, often say to myself, 'How'm I doing, Corbusier?' You see, Corbusier was my teacher. . . . Paul Cret was my teacher and Corbusier was my teacher. . . . And I have learned not to do as they did . . . not to imitate . . . but to derive out of their spirit.[6]

Le Corbusier frequently based the proportions of his buildings, or portions of them, on classical systems of mathematical and

FIG 11: Second floor, Library Court staircase cylinder

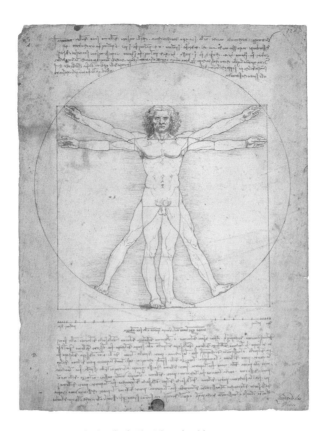

FIG 12: Leonardo da Vinci, *The Vitruvian Man*.
Gallerie dell'Accademia, Venice, Italy

FIG 13: The golden ratio

A (80 feet)   B (120 feet)

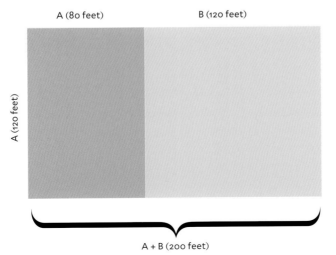

A (120 feet)

A + B (200 feet)

geometrical relationships that yielded a sense of balance and harmony, echoing what Kahn had admired in the architecture of the distant past. Le Corbusier repeatedly used the golden ratio (also referred to as "golden mean" or "golden section") to achieve the effect he wanted. He saw the mathematical ratio as a continuation of a long tradition that dated back to the Roman architect Vitruvius, carried forward famously by Leonardo da Vinci in his drawing *The Vitruvian Man* and by a succession of architects up to the present day.[7]

GOLDEN RATIO | GOLDEN RECTANGLES

A golden ratio occurs when the ratio of two parts of a line to its largest part is equal to the ratio of the largest part to the smallest. It can be expressed algebraically as the ratio of (a + b) to (the larger of a or b). A golden rectangle is formed when the sides of the rectangle are in the golden ratio. The golden ratio and golden rectangles were fundamental to Kahn's creation of the Center.

The Center, in plan, is 200 feet by 120 feet on a 20-foot square-bay system. The building is a golden rectangle in that if the plan is divided by dropping a line along the long side at 120 feet (the length of the short side), it creates a 120-foot square.

Similar squares and golden rectangles repeat throughout the building horizontally and vertically, creating or approximating different regular shapes in combination, including the relationship of the circular plan of the cylinder and the squares/lozenges of the utility shafts. The two mechanical shafts in the center of the building on the lower floors measure 20 feet diagonally from corner to opposite corner, a slightly reduced echo of a bay that has been revolved 45 degrees. Inside, the 20-foot square-bay walls are 12 feet high, repeating the 5:3 ratio in relation to the floor. Multiple additional instances can be cited but rarely with mathematical or geometrical precision. Kahn was an intuitive architect and followed what felt right to him rather than slavishly adhering to numerical exactitude. The Library Court, including the staircase cylinder, is approximately 60 feet by 40 feet, also a golden rectangle. Its plan, excluding the cylinder, is a four-bay square, 40 feet by 40 feet, within

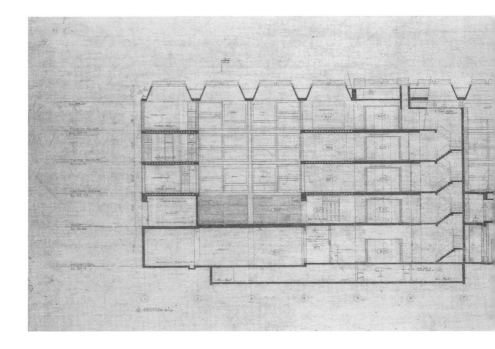

the golden rectangle, echoing the Entrance Portico and Entrance Court in plan—as does the adjoining two-bay plan of the elevator lobby and the staircase cylinder.

A standard 20-foot square bay, as on the second floor, could accommodate the circular staircase and entranceway—as it could the rectangular mechanical shaft set on its diameter (20 feet). If the three sets of treads in the circle of the staircase were to continue all the way around, they would form a pentagon (echoing the golden ratio of the building itself). If one envisions the circle of the staircase atop the square of the mechanical shaft, the stairs could represent an abstract rendering of *The Vitruvian Man* (see fig. 15), with the head, feet, and hands touching the square when the limbs are perpendicular and touching the circle when the arms are raised and legs spread.

The horizontal Library Court, including its balconies, rises the full height of the building from the second floor, an echo and counterpoint to the vertical Entrance Court. The rectangular building thus contains two large rectangular boxes.

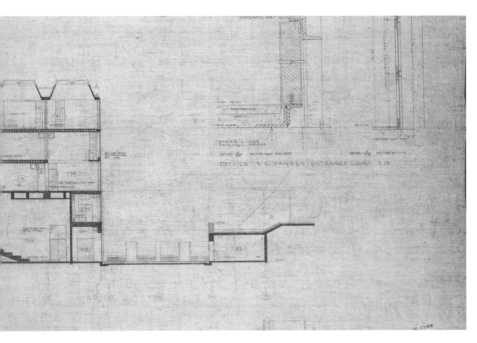

FIG 14: Second project, longitudinal section drawing, April 3, 1974, Entrance Court and Library Court. Louis I. Kahn Collection, The University of Pennsylvania and the Pennsylvania Historical and Museum Commission

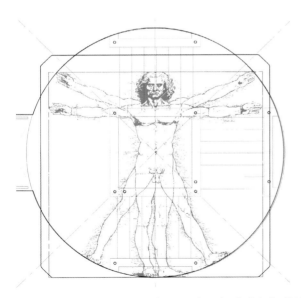

FIG 15: *The Vitruvian Man* in staircase and mechanical shaft of Yale Center for British Art. Knight Architecture, LLC, New Haven, Connecticut

CODE

*And you are saying that what you do now must bear muster
a billion years from now because it's reflective of the truth.
But beauty is something much, much more primitive. It is
the first feeling of man. The first feeling of man was beauty.
If I were to explain it, I just couldn't. I just believe it has to
do with faith.*

The Library Court is the heart of the Center. When I walk to my office
in the Reference Library stacks, I pass through a corner of the Court.
Invariably I pause there, feeling the presence of the Court before
entering it physically or, more often, empathetically. I, like other
visitors, describe the experience to myself as a spiritual one, akin to
entering a cathedral or a church.

*In the feeling that what is has always been, there is the
sense not so much of beauty as it is truth.*

"Spiritual" and "spirituality" were words that Kahn rejected
when describing the qualities for an architect to bring across
the Threshold from Silence into Light. They refer to an interior
experience, and it is not possible to know whether one person's
feeling is the same as that of someone else. Kahn preferred to
use code words to describe the process, specifically in this case
"common" and "commonness," which implicitly meant a shared
experience.

*The personal code is private. . . . I realize it when things are
played back to me that I've said, and I cannot understand.
. . . Though I know perfectly well what I intended to say. Now,
I must therefore find the . . . closest next word. . . . an inner
word which means something to you, which you don't
realize means [something different] to everybody else. . . .
But if you would ask me what I mean, and what you mean,
the difference is just worlds apart.*

Kahn achieved "commonness" in multiple ways and superbly in the Center's Library Court. The total effect within the space is serenity, the serenity of classical architecture, in the basic geometric forms of ancient temples and monuments.

FIG 16: Second floor, entering Library Court from stairwell cylinder on Reference Library side

STREETS

I felt the street, it's really the first community building. . . . It has its reason deeply in the nature of the making of American cities. . . . The street is the community room of the buildings around it.

Kahn was deeply interested in streets and their relationship to the city, in the buildings that border and define them. He believed that the lower floors of a building should be given over to the street and hence to the city.

The meetinghouse is only a roofed over street.

I think there's a lot of validity in making the first floors—I don't care if it is one floor or two floors—belonging to the street itself.

I would be completely sympathetic to having a building begin somehow not on the first level . . . the street as being sort of a breathing level of all people.

Kahn also gave particular thought to the commercial activity along the street, exemplified by the shop spaces surrounding the Center.

You design your street starting the street at the same time you are designing the building. And because also there were shops before, because you know shops only do well as shops if the stream of people that pass them is not broken.

I'm trying to make a shop more 'shop' than they are 'a shop.'

I don't want . . . the shops to support the building above. I want them placed . . . as though it were a little stage house . . . completely independent of the structure above, as though it belonged to the street and placed in the harbor of the protection of the building itself.

Kahn felt that streets belong to people, not vehicles. He felt that cars did not belong on city streets, in transit or parked. His ambitious, unbuilt plans for thoroughfares and large parking garages in Philadelphia attest to the attention that he devoted to this problem. Philadelphia lacks many of the projects that Kahn designed because they were blocked by officials who lacked his vision. He felt that cars should be parked beneath streets and buildings or in garages accessed via the upper floors of buildings, allowing pedestrians to shop below or live above them.[8] The architect César Pelli said that the Center was Kahn's best building because of its relationship to its urban setting, which would include the novel use of commercial shops beneath an art gallery.[9] Pelli believed that a building is more important than its architect and the city more important than the building.[10]

The Center's exterior has not immediately struck all people as pleasing, but it is a forceful statement of Kahn's architectural philosophy of Silence and Light. The opaque, matte stainless steel is a realm of Silence; the transparent glass admits and represents Light. Steel and glass, opacity and transparency have the same dynamic qualities as on/off—an appropriate and perhaps subconscious statement at the dawn of the digital age, reflecting Kahn's observation that a building expresses not an individual architect or client but a way of life. The facade subtly states themes of Kahn's philosophy—the golden ratio and golden rectangle, truth expressed in structure and materials, matter as spent light, and sensitivity to the street.

INTUITION

*If I had a mathematical mind instead of a mind which is
based on intuition, and I wanted to accentuate that part
of my mind more than I did the intuitive, I would find in my
mind what is now unfamiliar.*

Glimpses of the larger realm, of eternity, are achieved through
beauty, faith, religion, and spirituality—not through architecture
alone. Kahn's affection for ruins, buildings reduced to their aspiration
without the compromise of necessity, reflected his sense that a
properly built room would tell you what it wanted to be. He defined
himself as an intuitive architect.

Much has been made of the fact that the Center, Kahn's last building,
stands across Chapel Street from his first major commission, the Yale
University Art Gallery, and is thus instructive about the trajectory of
his career. Kahn, of course not knowing that the Center would be his
final building, never thought of the two buildings in dialogue.[11] Kahn's
more serious conversation was with the Yale Art and Architecture
Building, designed by Paul Rudolph and located diagonally farther
down the block, at the corner of Chapel and York Streets, across from
the west side of the Art Gallery.

Rudolph's building . . . has, in a sense, very willful things in it.

*He is just making this without giving nature any duties.
That's why he is not looking for order in any way. . . . It's
completely devoid of respect for nature's power which can
reveal order to you, which would never make a beam come
to a column once this way and another time this way, where
a beam comes to the side of a column and then in the same
building comes on top of it. . . . I am not rigid about how the
order is employed, but I am conscious of the order.*

Rudolph's building to me is like a crumpled piece of paper. And it is made in a highly circumstantial way in which every opportunity for it, but may have been a thought in the course of its making, was recorded. Nevertheless, the mind and the opportunity architecturally sort of came together and took hold of not allowing, which occurs to me, of the many ideas [that] fall by the wayside in favor of a consistent sort of note that runs through.

FIG 17: Paul Rudolph Hall (formerly Art and Architecture Building) at the corner of Chapel Street and York Street, Yale University, New Haven, Connecticut, 1959–1963. Architect: Paul Rudolph. Yale University Library, Manuscripts and Archives

Kahn's disdain for Rudolph's building is reflected in the presentation drawing he made for the Center. By use of perspective in the drawing, he made the Rudolph building look diminutive, but in actuality he quietly established his point about the superiority of his architecture and architectural philosophy—with the serenity and balance of golden proportions.

In 1973, after the forms had been set in the sloping hole that later became the Lecture Hall, I walked down and stood where I knew there would soon be a lectern where I someday might be lecturing. I was immediately and powerfully struck by the perfection of the proportions. They were just right. Perfect proportions throughout is the way that the completed building works. They are the reason why the interior strikes visitors so favorably and why the Center provides an ideal environment for viewing works of art.

FIG 18: Second project, perspective drawing, exterior view from corner of High Street and Chapel Street. Architect: Louis I. Kahn, 1971. Louis I. Kahn Collection, The University of Pennsylvania and the Pennsylvania Historical and Museum Commission

NOTES

1. Jules David Prown and Karen E. Denavit, eds., *Louis I. Kahn in Conversation: Interviews with John W. Cook and Heinrich Klotz, 1969–70* (New Haven and London: Yale University Press, 2015), 60, 78.

2. Louis Kahn, "Silence and Light," in *Louis Kahn: Essential Texts*, ed. Robert Twombly (New York: W. W. Norton, 2003), 236.

3. For Kahn's definition of room, see Prown and Denavit, *Louis I. Kahn in Conversation*, 195–204.

4. For a description of the skylight system, see Jules David Prown, "The Architecture of the Yale Center for British Art," *Apollo* 105, no. 182 (April 1977): 236–37; and Jules David Prown, "Lux et Veritas: Louis Kahn's Last Creation," *Apollo* 165, no. 542 (April 2007): 46–51.

5. For a description of the effect of the golden light in the Library Court, see Michael Cadwell, "The Yale Center for British Art, Yellow Light and Blue Shadow," chap. 4 in *Strange Details* (Cambridge, MA, and London: MIT Press, 2007).

6. Louis Kahn, "How'm I Doing, Corbusier?," interview by Patricia McLaughlin, *The Pennsylvania Gazette* 71, no. 3 (December 1972): 22.

7. For a more extended discussion of Le Corbusier's use of the golden ratio and other mathematical systems, see Le Corbusier, *The Modulor: A Harmonious Measure to the Human Scale, Universally Applicable to Architecture and Mechanics* (1954; repr., Basel: Birkhäuser, 2000), esp. 25 and 35, cited in Richard Padovan, *Proportion: Science, Philosophy, Architecture* (London: E and FN Spon; New York: Taylor and Francis, 1999), 320 and 324; and Le Corbusier, *The Modulor*, 130.

8. For Kahn's unrealized plans for Philadelphia, see "Monument? Forum? Fair? Louis Kahn, Edmund Bacon, and Philadelphia," in *Louis Kahn: The Power of Architecture*, ed. Mateo Kries, Jochen Eisenbrand, and Stanislaus von Moos (Weil am Rhein, Germany: Vitra Design Museum, 2012), 25–57. This volume was published in conjunction with an exhibition of the same name at the Vitra Design Museum, in cooperation with the Architectural Archives of the University of Pennsylvania, Philadelphia, and the Nederlands Architectuurinstituut, Rotterdam, July 9–October 12, 2014.

9. César Pelli made this comment at a public event at the Yale School of Architecture in Rudolph Hall on April 7, 2015, during an onstage conversation between Jules Prown and Alec Purves, organized for the book launch of *Louis I. Kahn in Conversation: Interviews with John W. Cook and Heinrich Klotz, 1969–70.*

10. Ann C. Sullivan, "Pelli Wins AIA Gold Medal," *Architecture* 84, no. 1 (January 1995): 23.

11. When I worked with Kahn on the Center, we would, at times, go to the Yale University Art Gallery to check something, such as the way light would enter from the north into the Gallery's print study room, which was situated in the same relative location as the prints and drawings study room in the Center. When we entered, Kahn would never look about him at his former work, in part because he was unhappy with the changes that had been wrought by the director, Andrew Ritchie, who covered the walls, windows, and circular staircase with plasterboard. Ritchie had done so to enable the display of more pictures, but also because he wanted to replicate the character of the Museum of Modern Art (MoMA) in New York, where he had previously been chief curator. Ritchie felt the changed appearance would attract the financial support of donors, some of them Yale alumni, who had been generous to MoMA. It did, and the Gallery flourished under his directorship, even as it suffered in terms of architectural purity and quality. Paul Rudolph had assisted Ritchie in making the alterations, which did not endear him to Kahn.

FIG 19: Fourth-floor landing at the top of the cylindrical staircase

Acknowledgments

In producing this slim but comprehensive summary of Louis I. Kahn's architectural philosophy—as materially expressed in his final building, the Yale Center for British Art, New Haven, Connecticut—I received steady and cheerful support from a number of colleagues, both from within and outside of the Center. The initial encouragement I received from Amy Meyers, the Center's former director, was extended by the current director, Courtney J. Martin. I am grateful to them both.

George Knight and Nikolaos Marchio provided me with valuable detailed, measured drawings of plans and also with new images that supported and embodied my thoughts and interpretations. In Kahn's terms, these materials brought my ideas from "Silence into Light."

Photographs are essential to this text as visual footnotes, as sources for the observations and ideas set forth. I obtained a number of them from the Louis I. Kahn Collection, which is on permanent loan from the Pennsylvania Historical and Museum Commission to the Architectural Archives of the University of Pennsylvania, the primary source for all things that illuminate the world of Louis Kahn. I am obligated to the archivists there for their help, as all Kahn scholars inevitably are.

For the superb photographs made especially for this book, I am particularly indebted to the Center's photographer Richard Caspole, who, often on short notice, produced new images to illustrate details and perspectives I discuss in the text. Melissa Gold Fournier was consistently helpful in locating useful existing images; Shaunee Cole insured that the best images were obtained and permission to publish them granted; and Lyn Bell Rose produced, as always, a beautifully designed book.

The book's production and editing processes were overseen with customary efficiency and precision by Nathan Flis, Head of Exhibitions and Publications at the Center, and his associate, Deborah Cannarella, Development Editor and Publications Manager.

My final and greatest thanks go to Karen Denavit, who has been my constant support from the beginning of this project to the end. She resolved all technical problems, detected factual errors, kept impeccable records, and produced essential data sheets that enabled the writing to proceed expeditiously. If this book is well received, much of the credit goes to her; if faults or errors are found, the responsibility is mine.

Jules David Prown
September 2020

Unless otherwise indicated in individual notes, *Louis I. Kahn in Conversation: Interviews with John W. Cook and Heinrich Klotz*, edited by Jules David Prown and Karen E. Denavit (New Haven and London: Yale University Press, 2015), is the source for all the Kahn quotations included throughout this book. In the list below, the page number on which each quotation appears is followed by the page number of the source. When there are multiple quotations on the page, they are listed in sequential order.

Page 6: 33
Page 7: 33, 26, 26
Page 8: 45, 45, 36, 67
Page 9: 61, 78, 34, 78, 75, 76
Page 10: 24
Page 15: 59, 59, 61
Page 16: 260
Page 20: 120
Page 23: 25, 25, 25
Page 28: 207, 207, 36–37
Page 30: 136, 154, 30, 31, 140, 140, 141
Page 32: 99, 85, 86, 139
Page 33: 139

FURTHER READING

Brownlee, David B., and David G. DeLong. *Louis I. Kahn: In the Realm of Architecture*. Los Angeles: Museum of Contemporary Art; New York: Rizzoli, 1991.

Kries, Mateo, Jochen Eisenbrand, and Stanislaus von Moos, eds. *Louis Kahn: The Power of Architecture*. Weil am Rhein, Germany: Vitra Design Museum, 2012.

Leslie, Thomas. *Louis I. Kahn: Building Art, Building Science*. New York: George Braziller, 2005.

McCarter, Robert. *Louis I. Kahn*. London and New York: Phaidon, 2005.

Prown, Jules David, and Karen E. Denavit, eds. *Louis I. Kahn in Conversation: Interviews with John W. Cook and Heinrich Klotz, 1969–70*. New Haven and London: Yale University Press, 2015.

Tyng, Alexandra. *Beginnings: Louis I. Kahn's Philosophy of Architecture*. New York: John Wiley and Sons, 1984. [Written by Kahn's daughter, this scholarly volume deals effectively with the architect's philosophy; the book began as an undergraduate thesis at Harvard-Radcliffe University.]

Wurman, Richard Saul, ed. *What Will Be Has Always Been: The Words of Louis I. Kahn*. New York: Access Press; Rizzoli International Publications, 1986.

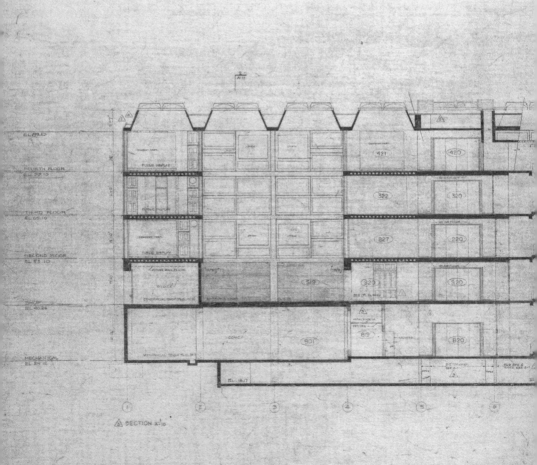